A DANCER'S DIARY:

Around the World in Thirteen Dances

by

To my soul sista
♥ Happy dancing
Dina
McDermott

DINA MCDERMOTT

A Dancer's Diary:
Around the World in Thirteen Dances
Copyright © 2017 Dina McDermott

Book and Cover Design:

Vladimir Verano, Third Place Press

All photos in this volume used with permission

Photo Credits:

Front cover: Dina McDermott and Marty Ponte in *Mandala*
Photo © Shaun Parkhurst

Title page 1: Soledad Barrio and Noche Flamenca in *Antigona*
Photo © Chris Bennion

Title page 2 & back cover: Akram Khan Company in *Kaash*
Photo © Jean-Louis Fernandez

Publisher contact:
mcdermott910@gmail.com

ISBN: 978-0-692-88365-5

For Irene and Jerome

Amor vincit omnia

And Maryellen, Maureen, Nora, Michele, and Maggie

With love and gratitude

For Bou Frankel, friend and mentor

Wish you were here

TABLE OF CONTENTS

Notes: the countries listed denote the country of origin of the choreographers. In some cases, they also denote the location of the performance. Chapters II, VI, VII, IX, and X were originally published on www.criticaldance.org.

INTRODUCTION

I said to my soul, be still and wait without hope,
For hope would be hope for the wrong thing; wait without love,
For love would be love for the wrong thing; there is yet faith,
But the faith and the love are all in the waiting.
Wait without thought, for you are not ready for thought:
So the darkness shall be the light, and the stillness the dancing.[1]

~ T. S. Eliot, *Four Quartets*

LIKE TRYING TO CAPTURE A DELICATE BUTTERFLY, the art of dance enthralls yet eludes us. Like sand running through our fingers, it slips through our grasp when we attempt to quantify it. A dance performance can shock, inspire, bore, or perturb us, but, when the final curtain descends, it is gone forever, never to be repeated precisely the same way again. Dance embodies the elusiveness of time and memory, the impermanence of life.

As we tumble through the twenty-first century, globalization and the ever-widening influence of technology render the art of dance ever more precious and necessary. Dance connects us to humanity, and helps us to locate our unique identity within humanity. In this book, I highlight some lesser-known and distinct forms, styles, choreographers, and dancers, both theatrical and indigenous. Whether it be a specific Hindu view of the cosmos (Bali), an exquisite ballet tradition preserved in an isolated, socialist country (Cuba), exploration of identity/sexuality (David Roussève/REALITY), hybridization of Eastern/Western forms (HT Chen/Remy Charlip), the Jewish/Arab clash presented in *We Love Arabs* (Hillel Kogan), the raw tragedy of *Betroffenheit* (Crystal Pite/Jonathan Young), or the ancient spirit of *duende* in flamenco (Spain), dance is rooted in the corporeal, but aspires to the divine. Join me on this terpsichorean journey, and together we will explore the sublime panoply of human movement—dance!

PREFACE

"That I became a dancer I see as a special gift of destiny. The dance, of which I was unaware, came to me, and I was one sleeping being awakened by bright, morning sun light."[2]

~ Kurt Jooss, German modern dance pioneer and choreographer

WHEN I SAT DOWN TO WRITE THIS BOOK THREE YEARS AGO, I asked myself, *What can I write about dance that adds a new perspective? Why write a book at all?* At first I was captivated by the idea of combining my three great loves—dance, travel, and writing. But the real, deeper answer whispered from my memories of many years ago. The first involved dance friend Lance Westergard and a meandering conversation on a muggy, summer eve when we served as dance faculty at a summer arts school in New England. Lance said his loyalty was decidedly not to one choreographer, company, or style, but rather to the very art form of dance itself. This seemed a lofty and ascetic philosophy and, in my novice mind, I was mystified as to its practical ramifications. My professional life was a jumble of auditions, rehearsals, and teaching jobs; I had not formed any personal artistic philosophy. A couple of years later, during a similar post-rehearsal chat in her Tribeca loft, Balinese-American Dance Theater founder/choreographer Islene Pinder humbly described her own body of work as a "small drop in the vast ocean of dance, but… an important drop."

I see this book as a response to and continuation of those two conversations from those many years ago. It presents an eclectic variety of dancers, choreographers, companies, and styles/ forms from the world over, spanning 1983 to the present, which I have found compelling, unique, and unforgettable: all contributing their own irreplaceable drop to this "vast ocean of dance."

Dina McDermott, Seattle 2017

A DANCER'S DIARY

Chapter I: Bali

Contemporary and Traditional Balinese Dance

New York, NY and Ubud, Bali
1983 and 1996, respectively
Choreographers: Islene Pinder, Ibu Masih, traditional
Composers: Anthony Davis and Epistēmē, traditional Balinese music, respectively

I. New York – 1983

1983, Tribeca, Manhattan, New York – I had always harbored a persistent desire to travel to Bali, and dance there. As a child, my love of Eastern dance forms began with watching the famous musical "The King and I" on television. This continued into my professional career, when in 1983 I was invited to audition for a New York choreographer/ethnographer, Islene Pinder, founder/director of the Balinese-American Dance Theatre and faculty member at City University of New York. Islene was that rarity: a Westerner by birth who had chosen to immerse herself in the culture of Bali. She had traveled to Bali many times to research the dance styles, and had even adopted a Balinese family, sending them money and care packages. I don't remember much about the initial audition, or Balinese dance classes held in her loft in Manhattan, except that the movement was fiendishly difficult and foreign to me. What I do remember is her frequent mantra, "Balinese culture is polyrhythmic." It would take me many years, and a trip halfway around the world, to fully appreciate this statement.

Islene's ambitious goal was to create an aesthetic syncretism between Western modern dance and traditional Balinese dance. When she performed the *baris* dance for us after rehearsal one day, she physically transformed herself into a fierce warrior, at once sacred and profane. We six New York dancers struggled in rehearsal to capture the essence of this distant culture. The resulting work, *Reflections*, proved hypnotic and seductive. It was performed to the musical composition *Wayang IV* (refers to shadow puppet theater of Bali) of composer Anthony Davis, whose chamber ensemble, Epistēmē, performed live with us.

However, in spite of all this inspiration, I had the feeling that the true essence of Balinese dance had eluded me. At the opening night party, a company benefactor vividly described the celestial beauty of Bali, which he strongly urged me to visit. As I basked in the glow of post-performance euphoria, I stared dreamily out at the loft windows of lower Manhattan. An exotic junket to the South Seas seemed highly improbable. Bali was a world away, and much too far to reach.

II. Bali – 1996

August 1996, Ubud Village, South Central Bali, Indonesia – Since my experience with the Balinese-American Dance Theatre in New York City many years ago, my desire to travel to Bali and dance there had only grown. One day in Seattle, my then-partner Marty mused that for our next trip, we should travel to somewhere "really exotic." We both simultaneously shouted, "Bali!" Months of research followed — scouring guidebooks and searching through old copies of National Geographic. We learned that Bali is set in the middle of the Indonesian archipelago of over 13,000 islands. The size of Rhode Island, it is a Hindu enclave nestled in the middle of Islamic Indonesia; a patchwork

Hindu temple outside Ubud, central Bali. Photo: Dina McDermott

quilt of rice paddies, steaming volcanoes, black sand beaches, and humid bamboo forests. In Bali, their unique brand of Hinduism (distinct from that practiced in India and with a strong dash of Buddhism thrown in) permeates every hour of the day, every phase of life, and every rite of passage. The multitudinous Balinese gods are not just esoteric statues in a temple, but living, breathing forces of nature, which influence their everyday lives, decisions, and fates. Black and white checkered cloths are wrapped around statues to ward off evil spirits. Every morning, tiny offerings of flowers, sweets, and incense are burned on doorsteps and street corners. Hindu religious holidays, crop plantings, coming-of-age ceremonies, village births and deaths — all are occasions for major day-long festivities. We fantasized about taking class with a master, but decided to wait until our arrival to make arrangements.

Our arrival in Bali was a dream come true, notwithstanding the 21-hour flight to the capitol, Denpasar, via Los Angeles. But the tropical spell was quickly broken by the din of urban Bali, a nation apparently undergoing growing pains. As we stepped out of a taxi we were assaulted by ear-splitting, invasive noise. The sound of jackhammers, sputtering mopeds, unmuffled diesel buses, and tinny, canned pop music clashed with the calls of exotic birds and geckoes. We dragged our suitcases past rice paddies and sidewalk stalls selling a dizzying mélange of cheap electronics and plastic household gizmos. When we checked into our guesthouse in Ubud (the dance hub in south-central Bali) and inquired where dance lessons could be had, the desk clerk identified her mother, Ibu Masih, the proprietress, as one of the resident dance masters in Ubud. What luck! We arranged our class for the very next day.

So there I was, fifteen years after my experience with the Balinese-American Dance Theatre in New York City, standing barefoot on the blessedly cool, white gleaming floor in the open air pavilion of Ibu Masih's guest house, ready for my first master class in Bali. A diminutive dynamo, Ibu's bawdy sense of humor punctuated our lessons with her admixture of cackling laughter and strict discipline. Teaching barefoot, she wore a traditional stiff, raw silk sarong, with a batik cotton print blouse; her jet-black hair in a cantilevered, multi-tiered bun. Taught one-on-one, Ibu started the class with the "Five Basic" arm movements exercise. The hand exercises started out simply, then became more complex, adding eye and head movement. Balinese dance is highly detailed; densely layered with minute, mostly upper body movement — eyes, head, hands, elbows. Some faint muscle memory remained from my stint with the Balinese-American Dance Theatre. The somewhat familiar angles reformed in my joints and my hips protruded into the wide, asymmetrical stance as Ibu self-accompanied with her unusual droning hum, an imitation of the traditional gamelan orchestra which usually accompanies dance. Quadriceps muscles became fatigued since most of the movements are done in a plié. The movement was weighted, grounded, and earthbound; there is very little jumping. Ibu yelped with delight when she realized I'd studied Balinese dance before. Chattering chambermaids wandered by, dust rags in hand, to watch our class.

After we'd done our warm up, Ibu Masih announced I was going to learn the Welcome Dance: a traditional greeting to the audience at

Before class: Marty Ponte, Ibu Masih, and unidentified German dancer. Ubud, Bali. Photo: Dina McDermott

the start of the performance. It involved carrying a tiny gilt tray of fresh frangipani flowers, and ended with the dancer gracefully kneeling and throwing the petals (held individually between the fingertips) out towards the audience. Sweat slithered down my ribs. My shoulder and upper back were throbbing from the fixed stylistic poses: lifted elbows and wrists, my head canted at odd angles, fingers continually flexed back at a 90 degree angle from the wrist. As the choreography became more complex, Ibu chuckled and slapped down my errant shoulder, and repeatedly lifted my drooping elbows. The elbow and especially wrist muscles were stretched to achieve the extreme right angle flexion which is constantly maintained. The head and neck pivot and swivel in planes and angles not part of the Western dance lexicon. In addition to sharply bent shoulders, elbows, and wrists, the style also demanded hyperextended fingers that appeared to curve up with knuckles bent backwards. The dancer's weight was held low in a plié and grounded with the body weight usually

Dance class: Dina McDermott and Ibu Masih. Photo: Marty Ponte

shifted sideways, which gave the appearance of "sitting" into one hip. The dense, highly intricate movement focused on upper body — arms, shoulders, head, and upper torso. Unlike ballet or modern dance, there was no "reaching out," or stretching movement. It was done in a contained space, within one's own kinesphere. Circular head and eye movement were oppositional, multi-planar and timed with subtle musical cues, further compounding the challenge.

Leg movement was relatively basic: simple pliés, occasional relevés, a single pirouette now and again. I felt new neuromuscular pathways forming, as my body and brain struggled to replicate these totally foreign, but intricately gorgeous movements. Classes plodded on, a mixture of frustration and wonder.

Ibu explained that Balinese dance was generally divided into two categories: sacred and secular, those performed in temples and those not. There were many specific styles of dance handed down over the centuries, master to student. The *legong*, young girls dance, and the *topeng*, which features ornately masked characters ranging from refined and delicate to buffoonish. One of the most dramatic, the *kecak*, featured fifty plus men in a circular formation, utilizing drone-like chanting and mostly seated swaying. The repetitive movement is done over the course of several hours and can induce a trance-like ecstatic state in the performers. Ibu explained that the centuries-old dance traditions continue to evolve at the National Institute of Music and Dance in Denpasar. Graduating students must choreograph dances, taking traditional steps and changing them to create new themes and movements. In this way, Balinese dance continues to evolve.

Taking a few days break from dance classes, we traversed the island from south to north and back. Villagers paraded by in ceremonial garb: ornately gorgeous, colorful silk sarongs and tunics; carrying multi-tiered baskets of fruits and flowers. The acrid smells of burning trash (everything is burned here, from plastic bottles to funeral pyres) and diesel fumes mixed in a nauseating brew in the suffocating humidity of August heat. Each village in Bali specializes in its own specific art form: Sanur for silver work, Sawan for gamelan instruments, Amlapura for ornate textiles used in ceremonial dances, and Ubud for classical Balinese dance. In the Balinese language, there is no word for artist. Art is an intrinsic part of everyday life. Likewise, there is no distinction between amateur and professional artists. Villagers have many jobs — one

Dina at the Hindu temple, Ubud, Bali. Photo: Dina McDermott

person might combine roles as hotel chambermaid, silversmith, babysitter, chef, and village elder.

A few nights later in the isolated seaside village of Tulamben, Marty and I sat limply in an open air café eating our dinner of nasi goreng, a rice-based Balinese staple. After three weeks in Bali, we both had suffered the dire effects of "Bali belly," so we barely choked down yet another plate of this dish. We perked up when we heard the clanging, faint, unmistakable sound of the gamelan through the tropical night air. We eagerly pushed our nasi goreng aside, and bushwhacked off into the jungle like Indiana Jones and Marcus Brody on an archeological quest, using the clamoring sound as our guide. When we arrived in the clearing, the gamelan went suddenly and eerily silent. A young man, head hanging sheepishly low, was being loudly berated by the orchestra leader for some rhythmic infraction. We listened as the group started to rehearse again. The gamelan is both the name of this particular type of orchestra, and also denotes the style of music in general. It reflects Hindu cosmology… multi-layered, richly textured, repetitive, and mesmerizing. Sue Carole De Vale explains:

> Underlying Balinese cosmology and aesthetics is the concept of

"rame" (literally "crowded"). Rame indicates the heightened excitement one feels when experiencing coincident layers of meaning, colors, sounds and events…. Similarly, gamelan music consists of layers of related melodies that coincide at specific phrase points punctuated by the sound of huge gongs. Whether in cosmology, with its overlapping and interweaving concepts, or in gamelan music, with its layering of musical texture, the more layers of meaning something has, the more powerful it is considered to be.[3]

The instrumentation is strongly percussive, with gongs, mallets, drums, bamboo, xylophone, instruments made of brass, bronze, bamboo, skins, and wood. The sound was unique and quite startling to the novice ear — a mix of a wind chime and a cacophonous, clanging music box— metallic, percussive, yet mellifluous. It evoked a combination of an insistent heartbeat with slow breathing; the sounding of a gong signaling a new melodic or rhythmic line. We stood there transfixed, peering through the darkening green. We were the only audience at this rehearsal.

On our final evening in Ubud, Ibu invited us to attend a dance performance. This show was unique for two reasons. First, the dance performance was an all children's affair. This was fascinating for me, as the Balinese dancers here were the same age as my ballet students back home, from seven to fourteen. Ibu's granddaughter was one of the featured dancers. It is traditional in Bali for a particular art form to be handed down generation to generation within one family, whether it be dance, batik fabric design, or instrument making. Second, the dancers would be accompanied by an all-women's gamelan orchestra, a rather new and unique phenomenon in Bali. Every village or *banjar* sponsors its own gamelan, which has always historically been male-dominated. Ibu, proud of her membership in this all women's gamelan, laughed uproariously and then whispered the difference between male and female gamelans: women like to have fun while they play, while men tend to be stuffy, boring, and too dead serious. The show was in a venue off the beaten track, with an audience of mainly locals and seasoned travelers who knew that popular downtown hotel shows boasted mostly glitzy costumes, rather than the authentic art form.

The performance began with a greeting from the gamelan leader: a stately, gorgeous woman adorned in a sarong of multihued greens. The gamelan musicians were seated on the ground behind rows of long, ornately carved and decorated wooden boxes which housed the mellophones (their version of xylophones). The first dance is a *legong*, a group dance for prepubescent girls. The *legong* is a stylistic primer for all Balinese dance and refers to another traditional Balinese art form — the *wayang* or shadow puppet theater. These *legong* dancers ranged in age from seven to fourteen and were arrayed in dazzling swaths of silk in shades of vibrant orange, shimmering green, and pale yellow. I was dumbfounded by the complexity of the movement and the ease with which these very young dancers performed. Their thick, sharply drawn eye makeup and dark silky hair plastered

Traditional gamelan orchestra accompanying monkey dance. Ubud, Bali. Photo: Dina McDermott

to their heads reminded me of little wind up dolls or magic puppets. The performers typically had impassive, mask-like faces, with dramatic flashes of eyes and quivering eyebrows providing a counterpoint to the smooth, fluid shifts of weight in the lower body. There was a rabbit dance with much hopping, nose/paw rubbing movement, and highly stylized twitching. The weaving dance was earthbound, with stitching movement cantilevering from the knees. The masculine *baris* dance was a warrior dance performed with a kris, or stylized knife. Many of these dances are dramatizations of the Hindu texts, the Ramayana and the Mahabarata, depicting various gods, monsters, and warriors. At the intermission, I sat stunned and speechless in the audience. Simple movements and phrases I had struggled for hours to learn had been executed seamlessly by these young children. As a teacher of children in the United States, I know the challenge involved in keeping my students' attention and imparting even the simplest of movements. In my amazement, I blurted out, "How can they get those kids to do that?" A travel writer sitting next to me succinctly replied, "They don't have television here."

III. Seattle: Epilogue – Then to Now

Percussion music is a contemporary transition from keyboard-influenced music to the 'all-sound' music of the future... we can perform a quartet for explosive motor, wind, heartbeat and landslide... this has already happened in Oriental cultures and in hot jazz.

~ John Cage, from a 1937 lecture to a Seattle arts society [4]

Seattle 2015 – As I drift warily into a new century, I know the political and religious situation in Bali has changed. The bombings at the nightclubs in Kuta Beach in 2002 by Jemmah Islamiyah drove home that sad truth. In spite of inevitable changes in my personal life, what remains central is my ever present and urgent desire to choreograph, to teach, and to watch people dancing. I listen to my treasured recording of the gamelan and hear the polyrhythmic reverberations in my own life. Like echoes bouncing off a deep canyon wall, it is difficult to decipher their origin and hard to discern a melody. Chaos can coalesce to art or degrade to dust. Breath, heartbeat, raindrop and sigh. As I

Tirtagaanga, highlands of eastern Bali. Photo: Dina McDermott

gaze upon the bamboo thicket in my own backyard and let the music wash over me, I draw aesthetic sustenance from this elusive heartbeat of the gamelan, an insistent celebration of the vitality and mystery that is Bali.

Chapter II: Cuba

Ballet Nacional de Cuba – *Swan Lake*

National Theater, Havana, Cuba
June 20, 2014
Choreographer: Alicia Alonso, after the original by Marius Petipa and Lev Ivanov
Composer: Peter Tchaikovsky

"Are you the classical ballet teacher?" asked our tour guide as our bus pulled away from the Jose Martí Airport. "Are you interested in seeing the Ballet Nacional perform *Swan Lake*?"

"Sí!" I nearly shouted, levitating out of my seat. I was in Havana for a long, culture-packed weekend: a complicated endeavor, due to travel restrictions on American citizens, who may only legally travel to Cuba with an organized, state licensed tour for cultural or educational purposes. We were visiting art galleries, printmaking studios, recording studios, and other activities geared to our individualized interests. Sipping mojitos, whilst languidly lounging on the beach, was noticeably not on our itinerary.

As Friday night arrived, we eagerly entered the theater lobby and joined the line for our program. The carpeting was tattered, the lighting very dim. As we found our seats, I noticed some stagehands peeking out from the behind the curtain ... strange. Simultaneously, the audience around us was murmuring and glancing up and to the first, right balcony seats, while flashbulbs started popping. An elegant, slightly stooped figure in magenta sequined dress and matching head scarf was being assisted to her seat as applause rippled through the crowd. It was the legendary Alicia Alonso, co-founder and "Queen Mother" of Cuban ballet! A prima ballerina and star in the 1940s with American Ballet Theatre, she co-founded the National Ballet School and company with her husband, Fernando, which she still directs at the age of ninety-two. I felt incredibly lucky to be here to see such an historic figure!

As the curtain rose, the first theatrical element I noticed was the worn and dated sets. Material scarcity is the norm in Cuba. Due to the longstanding U.S. trade embargo, there are shortages of everything from gasoline to light bulbs to toilet paper. The dazzling backdrops and lavish costumes we're accustomed to in the U.S. and Europe are definitely not part of the experience here. But there is no shortage of stellar dancing and choreography — and in *Swan Lake*, the apotheosis of the Romantic style, we see the Cuban dancers at their purest, most luminous best. To see them in their own theater, with a full orchestra, in front of an adoring home crowd, is a once-in-a-lifetime experience.

Odette/Odile was danced gloriously by Viengsay Valdés, a ballerina of international renown, at the height of her technical and dramatic powers. She displayed an uncanny ability to contrast an ethereal, delicate Odette with the naughty trickster, the Black Swan/Odile. At the end of Act Two, Viengsay's rippling, seemingly boneless arms as she bouréed offstage, lured back into the evil spell of Von Rothbart, were truly astonishing. As Odile, she whipped effortlessly through the infamous thirty-two fouettés, liberally interspersed with double pirouettes. Legend has it young Viengsay would practice her balance until she could balance on pointe unsupported for one full minute. However, she doesn't rely on technical tricks alone, as her portrayal was an organic study in contrasts.

Old Havana, Cuba. Photo: Darla Mosse

National Theater, Havana, Cuba. Photo: Dina McDermott

Victor Estevez as Prince Siegfried, while technically assured in his solos, seemed slightly tentative in the acting and partnering segments. One wonders if the recent defection on June 9th of six Ballet Nacional dancers to Puerto Rico necessitated any shuffling of roles within the company.

Interestingly, while the Romantic style is second nature for these dancers, the corps also shone in the character dances — the romping, stomping rhythm of the czardas and the lithe, haughty Spanish divertissement. The Russian influenced training is evident in their sumptuous port de bras and generous épaulement. They dance right down to their fingertips; faces alive

Viengsay Valdés as Odette and Moisés Martin as Prince Siegfried.
Photo: Rosalie O'Connor

and animated. This was typified in the Act One pas de trois, danced by Dayesi Torriente, Estheysis Menendez, and Alfredo Ibañez, but carried through the entire ballet. The male dancers excel in their soaring grand jetés, which have that uncanny quality of breathlessly stopping, suspended in mid-air. Clean, rock solid tours en l'air and precise foot positions are the order of the day.

In Alonso's version, the Epilogue presents an atypical twist to this classic. Prince Siegfried returns to the lake, hoping to redeem himself to Odette. The flock of swans blocks his pathway, as they are protecting and shielding Odette. The corps are especially menacing, a flying wedge gathered upstage left, bouréeing in place in fourth position, aggressively leaning forward from the hips, winged arms drawn back and shaking. One can almost visualize them hissing at and vanquishing the hapless Prince. Ultimately, in this version, the love of Siegfried is strong enough to break Von Rothbart's spell, and all the swans morph into "doncellas" (as written in the program)… an antiquated term, literally translated, "virginal young maidens." The ballet concludes with Siegfried and Odette reunited in perfect love, a happy ending to be sure.

Viengsay Valdés as Odile and Yansiel Pujada as Von Rothbart.
Photo: Rosalie O'Connor

The Cuban ballet audience has the energy of a football match. The fans boogie in their seats, whistling, stomping their feet, and rhythmically clapping to their favorite music. Ballet enjoys pop culture status and passionate support; everyone from taxi drivers to tour guides knows individual dancers by name. The arts, both indigenous and classical, are easily accessible to all Cuban citizens. This brings to mind a quote from contemporary ballet set/costume designer Jerome Kaplan: "People don't realize how classical ballet is important and part of our cultural heritage, exactly like Noh and Kabuki for the Japanese. We need to keep it alive and fight to transfer it to the younger generation."[5] The Ballet Nacional and Cuban society have warmly embraced this philosophy with *un gran abrazo* (a big hug). Long may they shine!

El Arenal, Sevilla, Spain
June 23, 2015
Choreography: Traditional
Composers: Traditional Flamenco guitar and vocals

Flamenco is an "art in three dimensions—the dimension of space, the dimension of time and the dimension of the soul." So states a display at the fascinating Flamenco Museum in Seville, the capitol of the southern Spanish province of Andalusia. The modern day beating heart of this ancient art form is housed at the Tablao Arenal (Flamenco Theatre in the Arenal barrio in Seville), which lies in the shadow of the bullring on the banks of the Guadalquivir River. On this my second visit to the Tablao Arenal (last visited in 2010), I opted to sit directly in front of the stage at a dinner/show combo. I wanted to have a prime seat to view the lightning quick footwork and feel the staccato rhythms.

Believed to have originated in India and brought by gypsies as they wandered westward, flamenco flows from the joy, pain, and passion of these nomadic peoples. The dance form of flamenco is related to the musical form *cante jondo*, or deep song. Described by poet Federico García Lorca in his singular treatise "Deep Song", flamenco originates in ancient Indian musical forms inspired by bird calls, the wind's whisper, and the rhythmic hoof beats of the gypsies' horses. Pursued by Tamerlane's army, the gypsies fled India in the fifteenth century, but flamenco didn't evolve to its current form until about the 1800s. The lyrical themes of flamenco/deep song are fatalistic and obsessed with the tragic dichotomy between love and death and the rootlessness and longing of gypsy culture. Somber dances such as *seguiríyas* and the fierce *farrucca*, contrasted with the bubbly *alegrías* and joyous *bulerías*, portray a rich and broad range of emotions.

Our flamenco evening began with a traditional musical interlude. Two singers and guitarists walked onstage in darkness and settled into chairs

LA PIÑONA, El Arenal, Seville, Spain. Photo: Alonso Espartero

Foto: ©Alonso Espartero

on a rather small, intimate stage. The guitarists played a nimble earthy riff and the singers trilled a guttural, poetic wail, accompanied by a cupped-hand, muffled clapping called *palmas* or *compas*. The male vocal technique is a mournful wail, reminiscent of the chant-like singing from two religions which have occupied Spain at various times prior to the fifteenth century: the *muezzin*, or call to prayer of Islam, and the *nigun*, a ritualistic, lyrical sung prayer in Judaism.

Maria Vargas, a regal blonde dancer, strutted out: her hair in a loosely netted bun, her ample torso swathed in a long, red-fringed shawl over a frilly, full-skirted red polka dot dress. She started the program with a bubbly *alegría*: a short joyful dance believed to have originated in the ancient coastal city of Cádiz. Next was a *bulería* danced by Isabel Lopez; evoking a playful, almost bawdy mood with whipping turns, deeply side-bending torso, hands slapping body, and explosive but precise footwork. Flirtatious asides between dancers and musicians punctuated the dancing.

The highlight of the evening was a *farrucca* danced by El Arenal's artistic director, ANTOÑETE. Whippet thin and intense, ANTOÑETE embodied this dance of male elegance and power. His demeanor suggested the matador: proud, graceful,

ANTOÑETE, El Arenal, Seville, Spain. Photo: Alonso Espartero

and fierce. His footwork was so hard-hitting that I could see the percussive sound waves lightly ripple the shawl I was wearing — we were sitting that close to the tiny stage! This was contrasted with slow, stretchy backbends initiated by a slide forward of the pelvis, again reminiscent of the bullfighter's stance. One arm would arc overhead, accompanied by haughty turns of the head and rapid twists of the body. I fully expected literal sparks to fly from the rat-a-tat of his footwork. He possessed what Martha Graham called "the gift of the gaze": a rare depth of intensity which looks both inward and outward. In flamenco, this is part of *duende*: a passionate energy felt by audience and dancer alike, the synergy of singing, guitar playing, rhythm, and dancing, the physical evocation of the gypsy blood memory. Nowhere was the power of *duende* felt more than in this astounding *farrucca*.

The evening finished with all five dancers onstage for a rousing grand finale: the traditional *sevillana*. Named for the city of its origin, the *sevillana* is danced by revelers in clubs, neighborhood bars, and at the traditional April Feria. It's a dance for couples and is similar in format to a classical ballet pas de deux, alternating between duet and solo sections. The couples whirl and twirl around each other: arms locked around waists, bodies plastered to each other, castanets drilling out a counterpoint to the feet. The typical haughty facial expression characteristic of many other dances is broken with joyous faces and nimble feet here with the *sevillana*.

Still feeling the vibrations of *duende* post-performance, the audience reluctantly trickled out onto the narrow cobblestone street, into the balmy evening air. Bathed in golden Mediterranean light bouncing off the pastel stucco buildings, swathed by the river, and anchored by the massive Gothic cathedral, Seville is often referred to as a city where it feels good to be alive. Flamenco, for all its evocations of pain and earthly woes, ultimately leaves us with a passion for life. Like the oranges that hang in the plentiful groves, its flavor is both bitter and sweet.

Guadalquivir River and Torre del Oro. Seville, Spain. Photo: Dina McDermott

Seville Cathedral. Seville, Spain. Photo: Dina McDermott

University of Seville. Seville, Spain. Photo: Dina McDermott

Meany Theater, Seattle, WA
October 23, 2014
Director: Martín Santangelo
Choreographer: Soledad Barrio
Consulting Director: Lee Breuer
Composers: Eugenio Iglesias, Salva de Maria, and Martín Santangelo

Combining the high Greek tragedy of Antigone *with* the quintessential Spanish rhythm of flamenco dance seemed like an ambitious project, or perhaps an improbable mix. But choreographer Martín Santangelo's Noche Flamenca group, with the directorial collaboration of MacArthur-winning Mabou Mines director Lee Breuer, set out to do just that in their world premiere, *Antigona*.

As the curtain rises, the guttural wailing of flamenco singing and guitar strumming fills the air. It would be impossible to overemphasize the power and impact of the haunting chant of these Andalusian melodies. The throaty, visceral sound hits the ears, drops to the solar plexus, shoots up the spine, and instantly plunges one into another place and time: a land of ancient ruins, the proud and often violent cultures of ancient Spain and Greece. As we bask in the timbre of this beautiful music,

stage lights start to glimmer and we see a haunting image: a raised figure, Oedipus (on stilts?), almost Christ-like, is wearing a 20 foot-long sheath-like stretchy robe, which is draped down to the floor. The fabric is shaking, quaking, and we realize that through a long slit at the bottom, out come the children of Oedipus; clawing, roiling, rumbling, and tumbling their way into the world.

This powerful image sets the tone for a complex story, one of the great tragedies of Western culture. Oedipus has died, and his brood is fighting tooth and nail for his kingdom. The directors present a very contemporary, vernacular telling of this ancient tale, with the warring children of Oedipus portrayed as a dysfunctional clan, à la *Modern Family*. The actors and dancers sit on stools in a semicircle facing downstage: feuding, chattering, and hollering. Antigone's sister Ismene drags her

Soledad Barrio and Noche Flamenca in *Antigona*. Photo: Chris Bennion

stool downstage while filing her nails, and speaks in Valley Girl slang in an intimate aside to the audience. Clearly she's the "bad girl" of the family. Antigone's brothers Eteocles and Polynices fight mano-a-mano and kill each other downstage. Their uncle Creon, next in line of succession, takes over the throne. For his inauguration, we get a procession of dancers marching in, buzzing on kazoos. Creon bellows his lines at the audience, evoking memories of brutal Spanish dictator Francisco Franco. The stagecraft for the first thirty minutes is a bit busy. We have narrators and the blind seer Tiresias speaking sometimes in heavily accented English, sometimes in Spanish. There are awkward pauses in the narration, with snippets of narrative phrases projected on a screen hanging upstage. Musicians scurry in and out. It's hard to know where to direct one's attention amidst the multimedia mélange. Distraction, not clarity, results.

The dancing part of the evening does not begin until about forty-five minutes into this ninety minute show. All this theatrical business is a mere backdrop for the main event of the evening: the incomparable artistry of dancer/choreographer Soledad Barrio. With Barrio as Antigone, we are presented with a thoroughly modern feminist icon for our time. In defiance of the patriarchal strictures of her society, she undertakes the forbidden mission of burying her brother, and will not be deterred by any impediments. When she first appears garbed in a raspberry dress, she has that quality many legendary performers possess; that ability to create an energy vortex around her. We can't exactly remember *how* she appears onstage, but when she does, our eyes are riveted on her alone, and although Barrio is just standing center stage, we are utterly mesmerized. Instead of speaking and dialogue, her character's strength is typified by sharp staccato footwork, the signature of flamenco dance. Snaking arms are thrust out from the shoulders and frame the head; fingers undulate and claw the air. Barrio, as choreographer and dancer, has made a conscious choice to integrate modern dance movement with classical flamenco vocabulary. With a lesser artist, this might prove disastrous, but because of her deep understanding and the tragic story, it works. There is a scene where the women's ensemble is sitting wide-legged on stools, doing a digging movement into the ground, reminiscent of Martha Graham's *Lamentation*. In another scenario, they stand squarely sideways: arms pushed out, heads turned defiantly profile, fingers wavering and undulating. They are telling a story all their own… a lament of grief, longing, and frustration. Barrio's characterization portrays Antigone as an archetypal female, honoring the warrior society in which the woman's role is to care for and maintain the societal traditions. When Barrio leads a snaking, ritualistic line of women, the imagery is stark yet sensuous, and again reminds one of early Martha Graham works such as *Primitive Mysteries*.

With roots in nomadic Gypsy culture of southern and eastern Europe, flamenco blends influences from Gypsy and Arabic cultures. It is a mingling of earthly passions, alternately joyful and mournful. These roots are melded into the spirit of *duende*, of which Soledad Barrio is the fiery personification. The most evocative moment was near the end, when following her imprisonment for burying her brother, Antigone stands downstage center. With a wispy gesture, she draws both hands across her face, gathers something (life force, identity?) together in her palms and casts it out softly to the audience, with all the poignancy of a sigh. With a lesser artist, these gestures would seem trite. Done by an artist such as Barrio, it feels astonishingly intimate. I thought of Emily Dickinson's verse from *Letter to the World*: "this is my letter to the world / which never wrote to me."[6] After gesturing, Barrio/Antigone then wends her

way upstage, a translucent scrim drops in front of her, and she hangs herself with a length of fabric.

Finally, I'm unclear on the directors' point of view and therefore not sure what to make of this production as a whole. Do the theatrical visions of Breuer, Barrio, and Santangelo really cohere? I'm not clear if I'm watching theater, dance theater, or high farce. Tragic moments were diluted by the broad acting style, awkward pauses in line readings, and guffaws from the audience. The almost cartoonish way that violence is depicted in the theatrical segments, the vernacular line readings, and the screechy guitar solo à la Jimi Hendrix in one emotional interlude clash jarringly with the deep, soulful spirit of the flamenco sequences. Although the dance and theatrical elements feel like two separate productions, the intensity and artistry of Soledad Barrio transcend all these concerns, and make it a production definitely worth seeing.

Theatre of the Riverside Church, New York City, NY
May 28, 1986
Choreography realized and directed by H.T. Chen, from a word and picture score by Remy Charlip
Composers: Excerpts from Eastern and Western popular and classical music

What do you get when you mix the whimsical, postmodern sensibility of choreographer Remy Charlip with the lyrically Asian, classically modern dance style of H. T. Chen? You get *39 Chinese Attitudes*. Charlip is known for his development of a movement process he called "air mail dances" (more about this later), which was reminiscent of the assemblage and found art techniques of Joseph Cornell, Robert Rauschenberg, and Jasper Johns in the 1950s. The latter two were set and costume designers who collaborated with Merce Cunningham, beginning with their initial residence at Black Mountain College. By contrast, H. T. Chen's aesthetic is more traditional, and evolves in a clear lineage from classical Chinese dance blended with contemporary Western styles of Doris Humphrey, Martha Graham, and Paul Taylor. The unusual melding of these genres seen in *39 Chinese Attitudes* is a fascinating and little known chapter of contemporary dance history.

Remy Charlip—an original dancer in the Merce Cunningham Company, choreographer, costume designer, award-winning children's book author/illustrator and Alexander practitioner— was an expat living in Paris. Friend and dancer Nancy Lewis, living in the States, wanted to commission him to choreograph a solo for her, but he was unable to leave France. Charlip came up with a solution—a choreographic process that he labeled "air mail dances." He sent Lewis postcards with drawings of figures to put together into a dance... to be arranged in any order and adding her own transitions. This transatlantic collaboration became a solo dance, which was performed at Dance Theater Workshop in 1980. In 1986, utilizing the same process, choreographer H. T. Chen collaborated with Charlip to develop a group dance for Chen and Dance: *39 Chinese Attitudes*. According to H.T. Chen & Dancers' Associate Artistic Director Dian Dong, Charlip had collected

thousands of fortune cookie slips and kept an entire drawer full of them. Inspired by these amusing

☺ Stop searching forever, happiness is just next to you. ☺

The index finger is moving, there is good food on the way.

fortunes and coupling them with drawings and dance photos, Charlip mailed the package to H.T. Chen. The piece evolved by randomly combining these sayings with action photos and drawings Charlip had selected. According to the program notes, the score for the dance "consists of Chinese paper cut-outs, historic photographs of dancers, sports photographs. An attitude is followed by a jump followed by a fall." Using this choreographic process in a suite of short, discrete sections, *39 Chinese Attitudes* is a hybridization of Eastern and Western movement motifs and cultural references; portraying heroic, amusing, and tongue-in-cheek scenarios. It is a dance for one man and four women, set to a musical taped collage of Eastern and Western songs, ranging from popular/jazz to Western classical to Chinese traditional/folk tunes.

As the lights slowly fade up, we hear the raspy strains of Louis Armstrong singing "Chinatown,

From *39 Chinese Attitudes* dance program, ©Remy Charlip, 1980. Artist unknown.

My Chinatown." Facing downstage, Dian Dong (the other four dancers are scattered facing upstage, statuesquely frozen in mid-step) solemnly and ceremoniously pulls out a huge fortune cookie from behind her back and slowly draws out the fortune slip. As her eyes slyly scan the message, a slow Cheshire cat grin spreads across her face, her body lurches into convulsive laughter and falls to the floor. Dong is joined by the rollicking group, and mirroring the trumpet riffs of Armstrong, they bound cross stage with giddy, jazzy spins, falls and rolls to the floor, and athletic jumps and slides; fulfilling the "attitude, jump, fall" structure.

Genevieve Lam and Patrick Gutierrez in *39 Chinese Attitudes*. Photo: Carol Rosegg

There is a dramatic mood change in the third section, a solo dance set to the rousing chorus of the Chinese classic "Yellow River." Less a song than a battle cry, it sets the mood for a lone woman warrior. As she runs the periphery of the stage (battleground?), her fists pump and her eyes flash like Joan of Arc leading an army. Her character reflects the history and mythology of women warriors in Chinese culture: from the ancient Hua Mulan who led an army upon the demise of her father, to the woman pirate Ching Shih of the eighteenth and nineteenth centuries, who challenged the British, Portuguese, and Qing Dynasties.

Next follows a giddy love-struck duet with Nai-Ni Chen (no relation) and Patrick Gutierrez, danced to a charmingly anachronistic vintage recording of Fred Astaire crooning "Not For All the Rice in China." Chen and Gutierrez swoon, swirl round, and cavort with one another in a postmodern version of a Fred and Ginger duet.

A slapstick routine follows with dancers popping out randomly from the wings; tripping, rolling, and tumbling across the stage. This segues into a women's trio, where we see the dancers clad in vibrant red unitards (with trim suggesting some kind of uniform), toiling industriously, simulating repetitive movements from field and factory. Gutierrez then entertains us with a hilarious solo to the familiar strains of the iconic Chinese variation from the Nutcracker. Gutierrez plays a foppish character performing gymnastic gyrations, spoofing Western stereotypes of subservient Chinese characters. The final ensemble section is all swirling, beautiful canonical lines with the dancers' arms forming filigreed shapes, folding and unfolding, as they ripple from one side of the stage to the other. The characteristic delicate hand and arm movements from classical Chinese dance trace calligraphic motifs in space.

Chinese visual artist Ai Weiwei, Korean video artist Nam June Paik, and American composers John Cage, Steve Reich, and Philip Glass are but a few examples of artists who appropriated themes, techniques, materials, and forms from each other's cultures. Straddling the twentieth and twenty-first centuries, their work attempted to transcend political and aesthetic divides. H.T. Chen is a dance exemplar of this artistic trend. Chen's body of work is linked to the classical modern dance heritage of Martha Graham, Doris Humphrey, and especially Juilliard composition teacher Doris Rudko; a protégé and assistant to the legendary Louis Horst. His movement style is uniquely beautiful,

Chen and Dancers, *39 Chinese Attitudes*. Photo: Carol Rosegg

combining the strength and athleticism of martial arts, the earthiness of Chinese folk dance, and the clean sculptural lines of Western modern dance. In an interview with *Downtown Dance* from 1998, Chen states:

> In the past 20 years we have been working hard to develop my own style. My work has a lot of my own heritage. The style is made up of two trends, one from the east and one from the west. Each trend has its own voice, but when they meet a new voice comes out. Like two instruments put together, it's no longer one sound or the other, but a new sound.[7]

In *39 Chinese Attitudes* we encounter the epitome of this "new sound"— a concatenation of East meets West, traditional meets contemporary. Since 1986, Chen's work has evolved to explore cultural history and identity in such pieces as *Shift* (2006), an evening length, mesmerizing, dreamlike piece with undertones of 9/11 (Chen's company studio, located in Chinatown, is roughly one mile from the former World Trade Center site). *Bian Dan* (2000) addresses the cultural and generational gap in Asian families. *South of Gold Mountain* (2015), distilled from extensive oral histories, explores the fascinating yet little-known story of Chinese-Americans in the American Deep South during the early twentieth century. But at its most profound, Chen's work looks even deeper than the immigrant experience and seeks a universal humanistic spirituality. In an interview with *Downtown Dance*, speaking of *Transparent Hinges* (1996), Chen said:

> It's more tuned to the spiritual and the ritual. The dance has five sections. It's the five elements in combination with the wind. I think the wind has a spirituality, like a wing to fly. The concept has a modern feeling … I just thought it was so important, spiritually, to meet the next century.[8]

UPDATE: Sadly, Remy Charlip passed away in 2012 at the age of 83. In a fitting, poignant tribute and as their "final collaboration," H. T. Chen & Dancers were invited to perform Charlip's *Twelve Contra Dances* (1980) at a memorial celebration of Remy Charlip's life at the 92nd Street Y in New York City. The New York Times wrote, "… radiant members of H.T. Chen & Dancers opposed and complemented each other's pathways through space, progressing from straight lines, right angles and basic steps (prancing, running) into more fanciful kinetic doodles."[9]

NOTE: Author was a member of the original cast for *39 Chinese Attitudes*.

CHAPTER VI: ENGLAND

Akram Khan Company – *Kaash*

Meany Theater, Seattle, WA
November 14, 2015
Choreographer: Akram Khan
Composer: Nitin Sawhney

What do film actress Juliette Binoche, the London 2012 Olympic Games, and *Giselle* have in common? Answer: they are all part of the artistic orbit of Akram Khan. Trained as a child in *kathak*, Khan encountered contemporary dance as a teenager at The Northern School of Contemporary Dance in Leeds. After founding his company in 2000, Khan rocketed to international notice, especially through a number of international collaborations, including with Binoche in *In-I* in 2008. Recently, he has worked successfully with English National Ballet, and is to create an updated *Giselle* for their 2016-2017 season.

For his own company, Khan's style combines contemporary dance and *kathak*.[10] He says he does not see his style "as a fusion, but a confusion"— a platform to ask questions, rather than providing pat answers. *Kaash* premiered in 2002 and was the first full-length work by Khan for his company. It

is described as a reflection on Hindu gods, black holes, Indian time cycles, tablas, creation and destruction. For this, his first visit to the Pacific Northwest, there was a heightened sense of expectation in the audience.

The piece opens with house lights on. Tall, lanky, and bare-chested, Sung Hoon Kim walks onstage and faces upstage, contemplating the huge painting of set designer Anish Kapoor, hung on the backdrop. He stands there for about five minutes, inviting us to ponder what the painting represents… a black hole, nothingness, creation, a higher power, infinity? Reminiscent of color field paintings, it is black and surrounded by a gray aura. Throughout the course of the piece, it seems to change color; sometimes looking like a window, a black hole, or vortex. At times it seems to change dimension or pulsate.

Akram Khan Company in *Kaash*. Photo: Jean-Louise Fernandez

The other four dancers appear and launch into a fierce, feverish dance: arms slashing and cutting through the air, legs lunging sideways to the pounding, propulsive score of Nitwin Sawheny. Their hand gestures reflect the *mudras*[11] of *kathak* dance, but the lightning fast changes of level and swoops to the floor harken more to the contemporary lexicon of Martha Graham.

After an increasingly frenetic, breathless twenty minutes, the dance dissolves into a slow, meditative solo for Kim. He is drawn into a duet with a woman who seems possessed or troubled. They dance as equals, leaning on and supporting each other in a non-hierarchical exchange of weight. More group passages continue in a ritualistic fashion, with quick yet precise movement, linear long phrases, and moments of stillness, accompanied by a score that features whispery voices and driving *kathak* rhythms. There is not much aerial movement or partnering in a traditional sense; the emphasis is on groundedness, fast changes of direction, and focus.

The dancers are just bionic; I can't remember when I've seen performers move this fast. I felt that if I blinked, I would miss twenty movements. Was it Martha Graham who called dancers "acrobats of God"? Khan's company seemed to fulfill this prophesy — one second in a spinning frenzy, one minute sitting primly on the floor with one leg extended, the next catapulting into a dizzying chain of turns and minute gestures.

Slowly, the music becomes deafeningly loud. This is when the backdrop appears to pulsate; an odd aural and visual illusion. It looks over them ominously, a force to be contended with. At the end, the dancers return to their original, perpendicular line with more slashing, pulling, and choppy arms. They have triumphed over some apocalyptic event.

I see *Kaash* as a ritual of the life cycle of creation, preservation, and destruction. These demi-gods of dancers toil through their ritual in a circle which continues on and on, reflecting cosmology as old as the Bible or the Mahabharata. While one magical, mysterious, or cataclysmic narrative is ending, another is waiting to begin.

Chapter VII: Israel

Hillel Kogan – *We Love Arabs*

Lincoln Hall, Portland, OR
March 21, 2015
Choreographer: Hillel Kogan
Composers: Kazem Alsaher, W.A. Mozart

When I read that Hillel Kogan's dance theatre work We Love Arabs involved "Jewish and Arab religious identity, national symbols and hummus," I was intrigued, bemused, and somewhat apprehensive. This is a hot, historically explosive topic. How could it possibly be addressed in dance? Israeli dancer/choreographer Kogan, who is also rehearsal director of Batsheva Dance Company, took on this challenge in his male duet at Portland's White Bird Dance Series on a mild spring night.

We Love Arabs begins quietly with a lone male figure in a shadowy pool of light. It's Kogan himself, in a one-legged balance, eyes downcast in a meditative pose. Slowly, the pensive moment dissolves and as the stage is bathed in bright light, he walks downstage, starting to sculpt the air with small gestural movements, speaking concurrently, narrating and describing his movement as he goes. We're not sure if he's a dance teacher instructing an imaginary class, a lecturer giving a speech on dance aesthetics, or merely an artist spouting stream of consciousness.

As Kogan's facile body carves and oozes through the space, his arms pushing, his back rippling and compressing the air, he muses "Sometimes I push against space, sometimes the space pushes against me. Sometimes the space resists me, sometimes the space feels positive, sometimes negative. The negative spaces, the spaces that resist me- I know these spaces belong to an Arab." I assumed he meant the land of Israel had once been occupied by Arabs. What could be a controversial statement is used instead to set a metaphorical framework for the rest of the piece.

Kogan wants to include an Arab dancer to make the space harmonious and to remediate this "negative" spatial energy. He invites his former student and Arab friend, Adi Boutrous

Hillel Kogan and Adi Boutros in *We Love Arabs*. Photo: Gadi Dagon

onstage to dance with him. I say "with him", but as it soon becomes obvious, Boutrous becomes Kogan's movement puppet or lackey. To keep their identities clear, Kogan invites Boutrous to write a Star of David on his T-shirt, and then reciprocates, drawing the familiar half-moon, star and crescent of Islam on Boutrous' forehead. Adi clarifies his identity and muddies the waters, by stating meekly, "I'm Christian."

The audience guffaws at the inadvertent cultural confusion. Kogan orders Boutrous to stay on his half of the stage, teaches him a dance phrase, then proceeds to coach him mercilessly, barking corrections—"more pelvis, explosive energy… MORE, MORE!" He coerces his friend to do a headstand as he holds his legs up with one hand, then proceeds to lengthily lecture the audience on the fine points of choreographic structure while he remains balanced on his head.

Boutrous finally launches into a sinuous, break dance-y solo, which Kogan grudgingly praises. Through this entire ordeal, Boutrous retains the hangdog, mournful, yet eminently patient mien of the perennial victim. He obediently attempts to fulfill all the movement tasks that Kogan foists on him. Dance folk in the audience giggle knowingly at the image of Kogan as control freak — many of us

have endured hours of rehearsal under the tutelage of a dictatorial choreographer. The pretensions, sarcasm, irony, and power gap inherent in these relationships are all played out onstage, in a playful, yet thoughtful way.

Near the end of the piece, the men engage in a series of cantilevered lifts, slung over each other's shoulders like a seesaw. Their relationship has become more egalitarian and cooperative. In the very last sequence, in an attempt to cement their somewhat common Mediterranean heritages, a bowl of hummus is brought onstage. They ritualistically smear each other's faces with it as the audience cackles. They then proceed to the audience. A large wedge of matzo is carried in, and the duo slather hummus onto bite size portions, feeding them to the audience members in the first row. We are left with almost a sacramental image, an attempt to create commonality and community.

Dance is about control—control over one's body, and in the case of a choreographer, control over other human beings—their movement, their postures, their very thoughts. The larger metaphor presented here is that beyond the foibles of the dance world, the "space" that is controlled by the state of Israel includes many Arabs. Like choreographers controlling their dancers, Israel

Hillel Kogan and Adi Boutros in *We Love Arabs*. Photo: Gadi Dagon

is mired in its dicey challenge: to navigate its role as powerful Middle Eastern state, U.S. ally, and a space where many disparate groups are attempting to live together in unlikely harmony.

In the post-show question and answer session, Kogan commented on his point of view and role as a choreographer, to "dream that you can make a difference in art…creating a bubble where we can sink into a fantasy that we can change the world. Artists have actually made big changes in the world."

Hillel Kogan has created that rarest of birds: a politically charged piece which is subtle, clever, thoughtful, humorous, and pithy… a piece that is relevant and relatable. In his "dream," Benjamin Netanyahu and Mahmoud Abbas could sit down together and watch this piece. What would they think? Would they laugh, would they understand? Would art indeed, be able to "change the world?"

Chapter VIII: USA

David Roussève/REALITY – *Stardust*

Meany Theater, Seattle, WA
November 22, 2014
Choreographer: David Roussève
Composers: d. Sabela Grimes (original music and sound design);
Nat King Cole, Johnny Mathis, and Ella Fitzgerald (recorded music)

Is David Roussève a dancer, actor, writer, director, or choreographer? He is all of these, but most importantly, he is a storyteller. His recent dance theatre work, *Stardust*, is the melancholy story of a young black gay teen named Junior. We never see him, but his text messages, such as, "I don't know u, but I text u my biggest secrets. Plz read, k?" are projected on the black cyclorama. They reveal Junior as a friendless misfit who has been raised in foster care after the death of his mother and grandpa. The danced story traces his life in all its harrowing, funny, and tragic consequences. As video artist/collaborator Cari Ann Shim Sham warned in the pre-show lecture, "Strap on your seat belts and get ready for a wild ride!"

In the meditative opening scene, Roussève's company of 10 dancers is grouped en masse, accompanied only by soothing cricket sounds. We hear their breath as they stretch slowly into a deep lunging backbend; fingers vibrating up the breastbone to the heart with a light, tapping gesture. Then torsos snap sharply into a twist, arms lusciously carving the air close to their faces. A soothing mood prevails before all the travail to follow.

As we read the projected texts, following the death of his grandpa, Junior is taken in by a foster dad, who plays a Nat King Cole record, then molests him. During times of desolation such as these, the character of Roussève/Grandpa appears projected on a small portable screen downstage. Like a Skyping guardian angel from heaven, Grandpa appears to comfort Junior: encouraging him, describing him as meek, righteous, and pure.

Stardust is a study in contrasts: the microcosm of Junior's tragic life story juxtaposed with the larger theme of human love in all its forms and foibles… unrequited, romantic, fierce, thwarted, humorous,

Kevin Williamson and REALITY in *Stardust*. Photo: Steve Gunther

Taisha Pagget and REALITY in *Stardust*. Photo: Steve Gunther

narcissistic, magical, and ultimately, transcendent. In a series of vignettes — some romantic, some street smart and sassy — the virtuosic dancers present a counterpoint to Junior's texted dialogue. The gorgeous, sentimental crooning of Nat King Cole and Johnny Mathis, the twinkling disco ball, and the celestial night sky projected behind the dancers provide a strong contrast to the brutal, harsh reality of Junior's life, and represents a dreamlike state to which Junior longs to escape. "When I Fall in Love" is a swooping, celestial solo danced by Kevin Williamson against a projection of a night sky. A nostalgic, floppy, flirty, lighthearted throwback group section of 1940s style jazz dance is contrasted with a more contemporary, street smart hip hop section, anchored by a knockout solo by Kevin Le to music by d. Sabela Grimes. In another section, Kevin Williamson stands with curved arms as dancers rapidly insert themselves momentarily into his embrace, only to immediately slide out and crawl backwards, allowing room for the next person. In another vignette, two women appear to be having a whispered, sisterly, intimate conversation, then scream in each other's faces, collapsing into giggles at the end.

Roussève uses recurring signature phrases and gestures to signal emotional states. Defeat and depression are signified by an ungainly crawling backward on the elbows phrase. The signature gesture of tapping the hand up the breastbone is repeated, connoting an individual soulfulness or essence. Grabbing the crotch in the hip hop section suggests confrontation.

Near the end of *Stardust*, Roussève (in the persona of Junior) appears in a riveting solo, danced to the iconic strains of "Ave Maria." Performed with an expressionless demeanor, the disjointed and sinewy puppet-like movements are a chilling reflection of Junior's wounded psyche. As Roussève crumples into a defeated heap on the floor, the story turns from dreamy to gritty then violent. Junior receives a text from a star football player, asking him on a date. After buying him a burger at McDonald's, the now predatory player lures him into the alley, and attempts to rape him. When Junior resists, his "date" hits him with a brick, killing him. The sense of inevitability coupled with sudden violence shakes the audience into shocked silence. The wrenching, reeling solo by powerful Taisha Paggett, superimposed with a massive slow-motion projection of a dove taking flight, seemed a bit literal and clichéd.

At the very end, the words "meek", "pure", and "righteous" are projected on the screen,

Kevin Le in *Stardust*. Photo: Steve Gunther

Kevin Le in *Stardust*. Photo: Steve Gunther

then the Beatitudes from the New Testament are superimposed over the words. Rather than a victim, Junior is seen as one of the "meek who shall inherit the earth." We are left with Junior not as a rejected and desolate figure, but as one of the chosen few… one of God's children. Although his journey has been a sad one, we do feel a glimmer of hope.

Stardust is a love story for the twenty-first century, combining projected text messages and mood setting video backgrounds with luscious and robust dancing. Although the narrative is conveyed by technology, the theme of love — raw, human, and ever present — is embodied in the physical, the dance.

CHAPTER IX: BRAZIL

Aspen Santa Fe Ballet - *RE: Play*

Lensic Theater, Santa Fe, NM
April 1, 2016
Choreographer: Fernando Melo
Composers: Zoe Keating, Ictus, and Blindman Kwartet

As Fernando Melo's Re:play *begins, a girl with a perky* ponytail in a shin-length tennis skirt and crisp white blouse (Emily Proctor) strides athletically across the stage, lit only by a spooky searchlight zigzagging crazily around her. The lights abruptly black out, cutting off her image mid-stride. Then the same "girl in white" appears back at the starting point and does her striding pathway again. Like a film frame run through the projector twice, the picture has repeated exactly. The audience chuckles at the visual déja vu. Midway along her path and at center stage, the girl does a stately kneel, lunges, and decorously falls to the floor directly parallel to the audience (she repeats this phrase several times during the piece, perhaps denoting some ritual). Men in shiny black knee britches and tunics start to crisscross the stage. One of these fellows repeatedly does a crossing pattern, hesitates, and looks back as though he dropped something. A tall, menacing man in a flappy, billowing dressing

gown (Joseph Watson) thrashes on the perimeter. An ominous feeling of missed connections pervades: dancers pushing against unseen forces and at times being controlled by them. All of this action is accompanied by a single, pinging piano note, creating a palpable tension. The mood is murky and disjointed. Various tableaux appear, then vanish, like flashes of a barely remembered dream, or images glimpsed in windows at night, mysterious and unknowable. I was sitting on the edge of my seat as I tried to parse a story from all these disjointed yet enthralling goings-on.

In one memorable sequence, Proctor stands center stage. For several dizzying minutes, the other dancers lunge at her rapidly from every angle... one at a time, spinning her around, whirling her by the arms, slipping and sliding arms around her shoulders and waist. Caught in a human revolving door, she is powerless to escape this vortex. At the end, Proctor repeats her signature crossing/

Emily Proctor and Anthony Tiedeman in *Re:play*. Photo: Michael Alvarez

Jenelle Figgins and Craig Black in *Re:play*. Photo: Michael Alvarez

kneeling/falling sequence. The searchlight flashes momentarily away from her. When it bounces back, she has vanished, like a footprint in the sand: there one moment, then washed away. Blackout.

Re:Play choreographer Fernando Melo (Brazilian by birth, European by training) has talked about the choreographic process of this piece. He stated in an online interview[12] that the dance was "constructed and deconstructed" with a series of timelines or phrases. The theatrical elements—lighting (expertly designed by Sean Johnson), music (Zoë Keating, Ictus, and Blindman Kwartet), and choreography are co-equal and combined in a "nonhierarchical way…. There is no story…"—but the final element of audience interpretation provides whatever meaning might be gleaned. In some ways, this is reminiscent of the groundbreaking "chance dance"[13] pioneered by Merce Cunningham and John Cage in the 1950s and 60s. It differs, however, in several key aspects. Cage and Cunningham's theatrical elements were combined purely randomly; there was no "collaboration" in a classic sense. The *Re:play* theatrical process appears more calculated. Also, the *Re:play* movement vocabulary is more emotionally or dramatically driven than the Cage/Cunningham approach. Like an aesthetic Rorschach blot, *Re:play* invites the audience to project their own narratives, fantasies, and feelings onto the stage action. Mine involved a wayward Alice in Wonderland, a postmodern version resembling an avant-garde silent film. I found *Re:play* fascinating, and look forward to seeing more from Mr. Melo.

Chapter X: Canada

Kidd Pivot and Electric Company Theater –
BETROFFENHEIT

The Moore Theater, Seattle, WA
March 19, 2016
Written by Jonathon Young
Choreographed and Directed by Crystal Pite
Composition and Sound Design: Owen Belton, Alessandro Juliani, Meg Roe

To the accompaniment of faint, mournful bells, we see a seated man, crumpled in the corner of a bare, harshly lit, institutional room. The stage setting is flanked by double doors topped with two windows, like looming omniscient eyes. We are in some kind of hospital, a suggestion of a man sequestered in rehab. Heavy, snaky electric cables are hanging from the ceiling and are plugged into utility boxes. The mournful man in the corner (*Betroffenheit* co-creator Jonathon Young) begins a conversation with disembodied voices which correspond to flashing lights from various parts of his cell like room. He keeps mentioning "the accident," says "it's collapsing," that he's trying to "rescue them." He is in a state of shock which has left him in a kind of suspended animation. The demons of grief and addiction then develop into a show within a show. This variety show has a wild cast of characters including sexy nightclub salsa dancers (Cindy Salgado and Bryan Arias), a crew of aggressive tap dancers (led by David Raymond), and a sinewy mime (Tiffany Tregarthen) wearing an old-fashioned sequined bikini with a tiny, clownish hat perched precariously atop her head. In a welcome bit of comic relief, Young appears as the host of this variety show, garbed in a garish blue leisure suit. Playing Young's alter ego or id, the mercurial and magnificent Jermaine Spivey performs with intensity, humor, and pathos. The plot is conveyed by Young speaking, the dancers lip-syncing, and bits of rare dialogue. The manifestation of this torturous internal odyssey is played out through the intense physicality of the dancers of Crystal Pite's company, Kidd Pivot.

Electric Company Theater's Artistic Director, Jonathon Young, and Kidd Pivot founder/internationally renowned Canadian choreographer, Crystal Pite, collaborated in this unique blend of theatre and dance—*Betroffenheit*. A German word, it has no literal translation, but suggests trauma and loss. Although there is a script, the piece is not theater in a traditional sense, but veers closer to the style of tanztheater.[14] The skeleton of a plot revolves around the main character played by Young, who has suffered a catastrophic loss. It is a window into Young's personal journey through grief—his strategies to overcome PTSD, and his attempts to distract, cope, and ultimately heal himself. The

Kidd Pivot in *Betroffenheit*. Photo: Michael Slobodian

story arose from a personal tragedy in Young's own life. In 2009, his ten year-old daughter and her two cousins perished in a burning cabin in rural British Columbia. Devastating and mind-numbing loss morphed into theatre. As written by Pite in the program notes, the work evolved "to use our art form to grapple with the question of suffering."

The piece's second half sheds the variety show theme and verbal bantering of Act I, and we enter a territory of fearless and transcendent physicality. The dancers have traded their garish feathers, sequins, and leisure suits for somber, faded blue and gray shirts and sweatpants. This section is a flashback or retelling of the tragic event. The sense of escapism has faded into harsh reality. Small, quick gestures of grief and comfort whiplash into astonishingly quick changes of level. Spiraling, death-defying leaps land in cat-like sprawls. A beautifully intense duet for Tregarthen and Salgado alternates delicate gestures of grieving and comfort with grand full-bodied movement. The Kidd Pivot dancers are exceptional in their range of skill (how many dancers are equally skilled in tap, mime, modern, contact improvisation, and salsa?), commitment, and raw physical courage. It is exhilarating to see the sheer energy and passion these five dancers bring to the stage. Young, the co-creator, playwright, and protagonist of the piece, though not a trained dancer, fits in seamlessly to the action. At one point Young is cradled and carried aloft by the dancers. Later, he is reclining with all the dancers surrounding, touching, and comforting him.

Betroffenheit finishes with all the roiling, breakneck dancing abruptly halting. We hear a bird chirping in the silence, and a disembodied voice says "you're rescued." In Spivey's final solo, he repeatedly bends over and does a cranking movement next to his knees, and then his hip joints, like a broken toy trying to fix itself, or a broken human, trying to make his way through just one more day.

The audience gave a roaring, standing ovation, with some in cathartic tears. I felt that the audience was cheering more for the virtuosity of the dance, rather than the tone of the piece, which was decidedly somber and tragic. As Pite said, "…no one is completely healed or rescued in our show…. Betroffenheit is about no epiphany, no letting go, no closure. It is a practice, a negotiation with the past."[15]

Tiffany Tregarthen and Jonathon Young in *Betroffenheit*. Photo: Michael Slobodian

Chapter XI: Native American Dance

United Indians of All Tribes –
29th Annual Seafair Indian Days Pow Wow

Daybreak Star Cultural Center, Seattle, WA
July 17, 2016
Choreographers: Traditional
Composers: Traditional Native American drumming and vocals

Native American dance has been a lifelong fascination of mine. As a young child, I remember my mom taking us to a Lenni Lenape pow wow in northern New Jersey. On a cross-country road trip in the 1970s, our family camped on the Rosebud Sioux Reservation in South Dakota during the heyday of the American Indian Movement. While in graduate school in Arizona, friend and mentor Peg Vissicaro took me to the Hopi mesas in northern Arizona to view their sacred dances. When serving on the dance faculty at Kansas State University, I invited Lakota Sioux friend Joe Medrano to visit campus as a guest lecturer in the dance and history departments. He was a professional Native dancer and had toured the world performing the traditional hoop dance. Recently, I was privileged to witness the buffalo dance, danced by the Rolling Thunder Dancers from the Cochiti Pueblo in New Mexico at the Indian Pueblo Museum in Albuquerque.

In Native American religion/mythology, animals and humans are considered brothers and sisters, descendants of the earth, created by the Great Spirit to co-exist in harmony. Elders and medicine men/women develop powers to meditate upon, interpret signs, and consult the wisdom of nature. Animals are considered teachers, messengers, and harbingers; sharing with humans important life lessons. Humankind must stand in balance with nature, not taking too many resources (trees, water, and animals) without giving back. Mother Earth lets us know her displeasure at any nature/human imbalances in the form of forest fires, earthquakes, and floods. The Native Pow Wow is a reaffirmation, a cultural celebration of these indigenous spiritual values.

It was with great curiosity, then, that I set out to experience the Native All-Tribes Pow Wow, featuring members of local Pacific Northwest

Cross-generational Native-American dancers: great-grandmother Arline Cailing with great granddaughters Keolani Caldwell, Calaiya Caldwell, Amanita Cailing. Members of the Yakima and Squamish tribes. Photo: Dina McDermott

Indian tribes. On a cool, overcast summer morning, my friend Tara and I ventured out to Discovery Park, which overlooks Puget Sound in north Seattle. Excited, we arrived early to stake out a shaded spot close to the front, then toured the booths featuring authentic Native jewelry, a colorful array of medicinal salves and teas, smudge pots wafting the scent of sage, savory plank-baked salmon, and traditional fry bread.

At the start of United Indians of all Tribes Pow wow, the master of ceremonies urged us to "look for the eagles soaring over, sending us blessings flying by." As we settled into our spots under a shaded canopy tent, the ceremony began with numerous speeches and testimonials, the most interesting being the origin of the Daybreak Star Center, on the grounds of which we now sat. In 1970, the federal government designated twenty acres formerly part of Fort Lawton in the rural north end of Seattle as "surplus land." Local Native American leader/activist Bernie Whitebear (of the Sin Aikist/Lakes tribe) and his followers tried to occupy this acreage in an attempt to acquire it as a Native cultural center. Through a series of protracted maneuverings, attempted occupations, politicking, negotiations, and ultimately a Congressional intervention, Whitebear managed to acquire a ninety-nine year lease on twenty acres of land in 1971. Today, an expansive cultural center sits astride a bluff and doubles as a museum, featuring Native wood carvings, painting, photographs, and beautiful community spaces.

After presenting the fascinating history of Daybreak Star, there followed much speechifying and thanking of volunteers, elders, and VIPs. We saw gorgeously arrayed dancers on the periphery of the crowd readying for the festivities. The Natives call their traditional outfits regalia, rather than costumes. They explained that costumes refer to dressing up to become or impersonate someone else, but in their regalia, they are signified as their most authentic true selves.

Before the dancing began, we were treated to a mini-concert by a Native ukulele band, which played "Don't Fence Me In" (references to reservation life and internment by Japanese during WWII), a stirring "Blowing in the Wind," and Woody Guthrie's "This Land is Your Land," with the personalized chorus "this land was made for Indians." Then various drumming groups were introduced, with such catchy names as Awakening Thunder, Spearfish, and Battle Axe. They would take turns throughout the afternoon accompanying the many dancing groups. Tlingit dancers of the halibut and beaver clan from Saxman Village in southeast Alaska performed a Memorial Dance, honoring "those who have passed before us." They wore the traditional conical, woven bark hats, and dramatic black and red wool capes bearing images of various creatures. The ceremony of potlatch followed with volunteers distributing gifts to all attendees—candy and small toys for the children, fruit and small household items for adults—all of which fortified a sense of sharing and goodwill.

The long-awaited Grand Entrance started at about 1:00 pm. The dancers were led by an honor guard, featuring a U.S. flag bearer, and another bearing the Eagle Staff, strung with feathers from all the participating tribes, including Yakima, Tlingit, Squamish, Duwamish, Puyallup, Colville, Spokane, Blackfeet, Tulalip, and Colville. Behind the flag bearers were the Fancy Bustle Dancers (men), with the signature bustle—a huge, ornate aureole of strung eagle feathers—strung to their backs. They dipped and wove dramatically —stomping, jumping, spinning, and waving, heads jutting and bobbing—as they clasped fans fashioned from huge eagle feathers in one hand and hunting bows in the other. Male dancing tends to be athletic and vigorous, while the women, as they entered second, were stately and dignified.

The most arresting feature of the women dancers is the gorgeous carriage of the upper back, head, and neck; the pride and elegance of their bearing, their grace rivaling that of the finest classical prima ballerina. They walked like tall, swaying reeds, yet each step firmly rooting them to the ground. The colors and textures of the regalia ran the gamut. The deep reds and blacks of the coastal Alaska contrasted with the almost iridescent, bright dresses of the Plains Indians. Adorned in elegant leather, fringed shawls, and intricately beaded moccasins, their jingle dresses covered with conical metal bells shimmered and sang as they moved. The end of the procession featured the children delightfully arrayed in miniature versions of their adult counterparts. The procession wound slowly around the periphery, then the dancers gathered in a circle for more speechifying, prayers, and acknowledgment of dignitaries and military veterans in attendance.

The playfully competitive format of the Pow Wow emerged. Following the Grand Entrance, the dancers were divided into sub-categories, delineated by gender, age, and style. Each dancer wore an identifying number, and there were judges who observed each dance and awarded first, second, and third prizes in each category.

There was a Tiny Tots number, Junior girls and boys, and Teen categories. The Grass Dances or Ribbon Dance originated in the Northern Great Plains; the stomping movement symbolizing the scouts stomping down the high grass of the prairies, creating a camping space for the tribe. The Jingle dress dances are performed by tribes from the Great Lakes. The fluted bells sewn to the dresses produce a jangly, pleasant sound believed to promote healing and wellness. The Golden Age Ladies danced next, dressed in their feathered and beaded finery. Known as Elders, they lend a sense of intergenerational connectivity and cultural continuity to this ritual. The Grand Finale of the day was the masculine, magnetic Fancy Dance, with the men bobbing and weaving, recapping their movement from the Grand Entrance.

As the sun set behind the Olympic Mountains and the Native voices faded away, we walked back through the mossy woods to the parking lot. We felt as though we were emerging from an earlier century to the current day, dazed yet peaceful. The Native All-Tribes Pow Wow was an enriching glimpse into Pacific Northwest tribal culture; one that honors the stories of its ancestors through dance. Our friend the eagle returned and whorled overhead, bidding us farewell.

Chapter XII: Singapore/France

Midlight, then we'll meet

Meydenbauer Theater, Bellevue, WA
February 19, 2017
Choreographers: Christina Chan with Aymeric Bichon
Composer: Lévon Minassian

Recently, one of my students remarked that in a happy, long-term marriage, two people become so close that they are like "one brain in two bodies." I was struck and a bit disconcerted by this image, but it has lingered in my subconscious ever since. Christina Chan and Aymeric Bichon illustrate this idea masterfully in their work, *Midlight, then we'll meet*; danced by Christina Guieb and Kent Giebel-Date.

As the piece starts, we first hear faint, lyrical, vaguely Asian chords, then we see a large spotlight beam in a wide circle center stage. A man and a woman stalk the circumference of the circle, each with a laser-like gaze aimed at the other. There is a tension, a feeling of confrontation, with the sharply delineated circle suggesting a boxing ring or athletic arena. They are wearing loose-fitting pants and tunics worn for practicing martial arts or yoga. The duo meets center stage. Like jagged puzzle pieces,

their elbows, knees, and torsos interlock, cantilever, and tilt; a foot balanced on a hip, a head peeking under a crooked elbow. One torso wrapped around the back of a waist of the other, their perfectly matched bodies wind and unwind around each other like unraveling spools of thread. Are they fighting in slow motion, or caressing? Pulled by a hand, or a foot behind the neck, or lying stacked sideways on the floor precariously hip to hip, their movement quality is purposeful, passionate, and intense: male and female performing as co-equals. The smoothness is broken by grappling clasps, hands reaching to arms and legs. They lift each other with a sense of weight yet ease. The endlessly spiraling movement induced a Zen-like trance so strong I could feel my consciousness slipping into a dream-like state. In one astonishing phrase, he crouches on the ground as she neatly hops her feet onto his shoulders to perch there, all the while he

Christina Guieb and Kent Giebel-Date in *Midlight, then we'll meet*. Photo by Rex Tranter

smoothly rearranges himself from a deep squat into a cross-legged yoga sit. She remains primly nesting on his shoulders throughout the entire maneuver, blithely unruffled. In another phrase, he squats low to the floor as she sits on his shoulders and reaches her feet forward to connect to and alternately press his thighs down, while he, sitting with legs outstretched beneath her, somehow propels them forward. They smoothly and rhythmically slide forward; a self-propelled human sailboat. At times, it is difficult to distinguish whose arms and legs belong to whom; they breathe and function as one organism. It often seems impossible to say where one movement phrase ends and another begins; indeed, there are no phrases in any traditional way. She cartwheels slowly against his upper back and waist; his arms nonchalantly windmill behind to assist her. This movement then melds into him cartwheeling over the front of her torso and shoulder, morphing into him cradling her, and finishing with her insouciant peek under his arm.

Initially, the partnering style in *Midlight, then we'll meet* is reminiscent of contact improvisation, a form of movement developed by Cunningham dancer Steve Paxton (and others) in the early 1970s in the United States. According to Cynthia J. Novack,

"The participants in contact improvisation have characterized the dance as an 'art-sport'…. The dancers in contact improvisation focus on the physical sensations of touching, leaning, supporting, counterbalancing, and falling with other people, thus carrying on a physical dialogue."[16]

Highly athletic and often virtuosic rolling, falling, and lifting result, although virtuosity is not necessarily the goal. It is a conversation, a wordless interplay between body weight and gravity. Contact improvisation reflects the social upheaval of 1970s America: a world rocked by the anti-war, women's rights, and racial equality movements. In contact improvisation, gender roles are demystified — men and women are assumed to be equally strong and powerful, with either sex capable of lifting and moving the other.

Although the choreography for *Midlight, then we'll meet* may have started with contact improvisation, it becomes something much more —the elegance of a man and a woman, dancing together as "one mind in two bodies." In the end, she slithers up onto his low back, wrapping herself like a sash around his waist. He clasps her tenderly by the back of the neck and the back of the knees, and they start whirling, two bodies, yet one vortex. The final image suggests the eternal masculine and feminine archetype... Adam and Eve, or anima/animus. Eternally linked and interdependent, they spin together into infinity.

CHAPTER XIII: GERMANY

Ballet West — *The Green Table*

Capitol Theater, Salt Lake City, UT
April 8, 2017 (World Premiere: July 3, 1932 in Paris)
Choreographer: Kurt Jooss
Composer: F.A. Cohen

I'm rushing through the airport, attempting to catch my flight to Salt Lake City, Utah. As I'm breathlessly running, I glance at the TV screens in the gate areas. The U.S. just rained down Tomahawk missiles on the weapons depot of a recalcitrant tyrant. In the shocked aftermath, diplomats are shown in the United Nations: red-faced, scolding, wildly gesticulating, and pontificating. Chemical weapons are mentioned, footage of dead babies are flashed on the screen. Was this an act of war? Was it justified?

I chuckle ruefully at the irony… history has repeated itself once again in a most numbingly horrific way. I am off to see Ballet West perform the most seminal of all anti-war pieces, Kurt Jooss' *The Green Table*. This dance is eighty-five years old, and I am wondering if it will still be as relevant in our twenty-first century era of drones, chemical weapons, and satellite guided missiles.

Choreographed in 1932 by the German Jooss, the dance was inspired by a series of pictures Jooss had seen at an exhibition. In the artwork, a Medieval-style skeleton dances with various victims—a beggar, a peasant, and a courtesan, among others. Jooss subtitled *The Green Table* a "Dance of Death in Eight Scenes," but over time it came to be identified as an anti-war dance. It premiered and won first prize in the Les Archives International de la Dance competition in Paris, and was recognized instantly as a masterpiece. Choreographed between two world wars as Nazis came to power, it was created during a period of massive political and social upheaval.

I first saw the Joffrey Ballet perform *The Green Table* in the 1970s when they were still based in New York City. The simple, archetypal characters, anchored by the doom-eager, skeletal Death figure, were seared into my memory. I jumped at the

Ballet West Artists in Kurt Jooss' *The Green Table*. Photo by Kelli Bramble

Ballet West Artist Chelsea Keefer and Demi Soloist Jordan Veit in Kurt Jooss' *The Green Table*. Photo by Kelli Bramble

chance to see Ballet West perform it in a rare U.S. presentation.

As the piece opens, we sit in darkness. The opening piano chords — spare, loud, melancholic — shake us down to our very bones. The score for two solo pianos instantly sets the tone of dread to follow. We see diplomats gathered around a green table, indeed reminiscent of our friends at the United Nations! They are bald-pated, garbed in tight-fitting tuxedos, wearing grotesque masks which render them comical, almost clown-like. They pace, ponder, pontificate, cogitate, and pound the table. They leap and cavort, miming gestures of supercilious concern. It seems that no agreement can be reached. They reach into their pockets, pull out pistols, and fire them into the air. War is declared.

In Scene II, the Death figure looms in the upstage center spot. Wearing skeletal makeup and costume, a gladiatorial breastplate and tufted helmet, he starts his menacing, stomping phrase, all clenched fists and slashing diagonals. With a menacing flick and drag of the leg, his hollow socket eyes gazing over his domain, he segues into an ominous, marching cadence. He flexes his arms with anticipation and delight as a regiment of soldiers leap, march, and gather onstage, rallying under their battle flag. They are pumped up and ready for battle, as the Death figure marches in place quietly and inexorably behind them.

A young woman appears, trailing behind her beloved soldier, about to leave for battle. Then, a clinging older woman appears, someone's mother. A slippery fellow tip-toes in: the Profiteer. He is the only one happily bidding the soldiers goodbye. He is elated at the oncoming war — he is about to get rich!

We are thrust into battle, the stained flag the center of action. Soldiers leap, tussle, and parry, but then are overcome, writhing and falling. Death appears triumphantly as a spectre among the fallen bodies. The Profiteer lurks in the shadows, nimbly stealing a ring off a dead soldier.

A band of refugee women drift onstage, mourning for men they know will not return. They cling to each other; they shift, sway, and skitter in numb disbelief. The Death figure appears out of nowhere and the Refugees scatter like frightened birds. Only the Old Woman is too feeble to run away. She seems relieved as Death picks her up lovingly and carries her offstage.

In the next scene, a young woman, the Partisan (a guerilla or a spy, these days we might even call her a terrorist) appears wielding a scarf. She kills one of the soldiers, perhaps in revenge. She herself is captured and shot by a firing squad, slowly reaching for Death as she falls in slow-motion. The firing squad slowly hangs their heads in shame after doing the deed.

Next we are thrust into a tawdry brothel. Blank-faced, garishly-garbed women dance with soldiers, presided over by the Profiteer (today we would call him a sex trafficker). The Young Girl is tossed around and dances numbly with all the soldiers. Finally she dances with Death, at first lasciviously, then tenderly. She melts into his arms as he carries her offstage. In her case, death is a relief and release from misery.

Tenaciously gripping his flag, the Old Soldier peers out from a foxhole, as Death crouches behind, a dark shadow. They link arms and parade; eventually all the departed souls join in the parade single file behind them. They do a stilted, hopping, corpse-like dance into a circle, then Death, with a scything motion, mows them down in slow motion. Later, the Profiteer appears. We think he too will succumb to Death, but interestingly — ever the slippery fellow — he tumbles offstage to survive until the next war.

Death repeats his signature phrase, then we are finally thrust back to the opening scene with The Green Table. Commencing this time with the pistol shot, the Diplomats return to the bargaining table. Oddly, although we recognize the same piano melody from the first scene, it sounds a bit different now… slightly "off"… tinny, almost circus-like. A lurid, dissonant tone prevails. History is about to repeat itself, in all its sickening familiarity.

The Green Table is an example of Expressionism[17] with an underlying influence of ballet (although the women don't wear pointe shoes and costumes are basically street clothes of that era). Although Kurt Jooss is considered an early modern dance pioneer (though he loathed that term), he believed the schism between ballet and modern dance was artificial. He also was strongly influenced by his teacher and mentor Rudolf Laban, who developed choreutics[18] and Labanotation (a comprehensive movement notation system that continues to be utilized today). For narrative purposes, simple mime conveys the story of the ballet. The beauty of the choreography is its utter simplicity and economy; nothing extra, nothing prettified. Meanings are conveyed in the most direct, non-clichéd way. The dancers must capture the clean simple movement without affectation or mannerisms, which the Ballet West dancers did admirably.

"In *The Green Table*, there is only war and those affected by war. The characters are individuals but also archetypes," stated Ballet West Artistic Director Adam Sklute. Jooss doesn't take sides or have any political agenda to advance. Most interesting to me is that the only figures who prevail are the Profiteer, the Diplomats, and Death itself. Although in the end we are left in a desolate mood, it does not persist. Jooss holds up a mirror to humanity, and dares us to take a long, hard look. We can flinch and turn away, or we can summon the courage and resolve to do better. *The Green Table* is his continuing challenge to us and the culmination of his artistic legacy.

RESOURCES

Anderson, Jack. *Ballet and Modern Dance: A Concise History*. Princeton: Princeton Book Company Publishers, 1986.

Copeland, Roger, and Marshall Cohen, eds. *What Is Dance?* Oxford: Oxford University Press, 1983.

DeVale, Sue Carole. *Gamelan and the Meaning of Indonesian Music*. Washington, D.C.: The Library of Congress Endangered Music Project, 1994.

Eliot, T.S. *Four Quartets*. New York: Harcourt, Brace, and Jovanovich, 1971.

García Lorca, Federico. *Deep Song and Other Prose*. New York: New Directions Publishing, 1975.

García Lorca, Federico. *In Search of Duende*. New York: New Directions Publishing, 1955.

Goldberg, RoseLee. *Performance Art: From Futurism to the Present*. New York: Thames and Hudson Publishers, 2013.

Highwater, Jamake. *Dance: Rituals of Experience*. New Jersey: Princeton Publishers, 1978.

Homans, Jennifer. *Apollo's Angels: A History of Ballet*. New York: Random House Publishers, 2010.

Lake-Thom, Bobby. *Spirits of the Earth: A Guide to Native American Symbols, Stories and Ceremonies*. New York: Penguin Group, 1997.

Lille, Dawn. *Equipoise: The Life and Work of Alfredo Corvino*. New York: Rosen Book Works, 2010.

Novack, Cynthia J. *Sharing the Dance: Contact Improvisation and American Culture*. Madison: University of Wisconsin Press, 1990.

Partsch-Bergsohn, Isa, and Harold Bergsohn. *The Makers of Modern Dance in Germany*. New Jersey: Princeton Publishers, 2003.

Robertson, Allen and Donald Hutera. *The Dance Handbook*. Boston: G.K. Hall & Co., 1988.

NOTES

INTRODUCTION

1. Eliot, T.S. *Four Quartets*, New York: Harcourt, Brace, Jovanovich, 1971. Page 28.

PREFACE

2. Partsch-Bergson, Isa and Bergson, Harold, *The Makers of Modern Dance in Germany*. Page 17.

CHAPTER I

3. De Vale, Sue Carole. *Gamelan and the Meaning of Indonesian Music*. Washington, D.C.: The Library of Congress Endangered Music Project, 1994.

4. Cage, John. *SILENCE: Lectures and Writings*. Cambridge: MIT Press, 1970. Page 5.

CHAPTER II

5. Jerome Kaplan, Pacific Northwest Ballet program, *Romeo et Juliette*, Jean-Christophe Maillot, choreographer, 2013. Page 16.

CHAPTER IV

6. Williams, Oscar and Edwin Honig, eds. *The Mentor Book of Major American Poets*. New York: New American Library, 1962. Page 196.

CHAPTER V

7. Diether, Doris. "A Modern Dancer Draws on his Heritage for his Latest Work." *Downtown Dance* 23 Jun 1998: 22.

8. Diether, Doris. "A Modern Dancer Draws on his Heritage for his Latest Work." *Downtown Dance* 23 Jun 1998: 22.

9. Burke, Siobhan. "A Choreographer Who Wrote and Drew." *New York Times* 29 Jan 2015: 24.

CHAPTER VI

10. Kathak dance – one of the several forms of classical Indian dance, this style originates in northern India, and emphasizes the rhythmic footwork (ankles adorned with bells) with accompaniment of tabla (hand drum). Akram Khan interview, Choreoscope International Dance Film Festival: Barcelona, 10 Feb 2015. < http://www.youtube.com/watch?v=h4h72Rd5lBg >

11. Mudras – A Sanskrit word for a hand gesture used in Indian dance.

CHAPTER IX

12. Fernando Melo interview, "Introducing *Re:Play*", Aspen Santa Fe Ballet, 26 Jan 2016. < http://vimeo.com/153138602 >

13. Chance dance – evolved from the work of modern dance pioneer Merce Cunningham and his unusual "insistence on freeing" choreography from dependence on music. In Cunningham's work, movement and sound existed independently of one another; choreography and music were both performed in space and time, but without affecting (or even acknowledging) one another. And most eccentric of all was Cunningham's use of chance procedures to "dictate" his choreographic sequences. Beginning in 1951 with his *16 Dances for Soloist and Company of Three*, Cunningham decided to determine the arrangement of sequence by tossing coins, thereby invoking a wholly objective and "impersonal sense of order, rather than digging deeper and deeper into some subjective inner sanctum" (Copeland & Cohen 310).

CHAPTER X

14. Tanztheater – developed in the twentieth century, a dance form which evolved from early German theater and modern dance pioneers, Kurt Jooss and Mary Wigman. It "mixed classical ballet to natural movement and repetitions with … a kind of ecstatic expressionism … introducing dramatic and compelling theater that was also dramatic and visceral dance." Pina Bausch and her company, Tanztheater Wuppertal, took the form to its most widely-seen and critically acclaimed level in such works as *Kontakthof*, *Cafe Muller*, and *Rite of Spring* (Goldberg 204).

15. C. Pite, email, June 8, 2016.

CHAPTER XII

16. (Novack 8).

CHAPTER XIII

17. Expressionism – a style of dance that "called attention to primitive drives that still existed in supposedly 'civilized' people" (Anderson 155). Expressionism in dance was developed in Germany by such greats as Mary Wigman, Harald Kreutzberg, and Kurt Jooss.

18. Choreutics – the relationship of the body to the space around it. Developed in conjunction with eukinetics, a formulation of all possible types and directions of bodily movements (Robertson & Hutera 78).

ACKNOWLEDGEMENTS

First and foremost to Brenna Arnesen, who said "yes" and went above and beyond to make this book a reality—everything from typing the manuscript, editing, suggesting, sizing and formatting the pictures, and a million details in between—a thousand thanks, Brenna. Pamela Rolfe, for being a friend through thick and thin, and everything in between. To Azlan Ezaddin and everyone at www.criticaldance.org for your encouragement and support over the years, and providing a home for my early writing efforts. Dean Speer, for practical publishing advice and help in the early stages of this whole process. Adam Sklute, Artistic Director of Ballet West, for generously sharing your insights on and experiences with *The Green Table*. Thank you to Joshua Jones at Ballet West for special assistance in securing photo rights for *The Green Table*. For Julie Miller, Steph Rake, and Darla Mosse, travel buddies extraordinaire, for making the sometimes harrowing journeys fun. Stuart Sweeney for urging me to keep my nose to the grindstone at a moment when I was ready to throw in the towel. Fellow Juilliard dance alumna Jeanette Bolding, for your friendship and urging me to look at the works of Kurt Jooss, a part of my own dance legacy and an important but often neglected dance pioneer. Laurie Griffith, for friendship and support over the years. To Tara Stepenberg and Nina Easter, for being my artistic sounding boards and helping me clarify my ideas. Katherine Raff and Pamela Boyer Thompson for initial help with editing. And last but not least, to all my teachers and students, for keeping me humble and still in love with this art form.

Photo by Gary Ryan

ABOUT THE AUTHOR

DINA MCDERMOTT has had a wide-ranging and eclectic career in dance. In New Jersey, she studied ballet as a child with Irine Fokine, then earned her BFA in dance from The Juilliard School. As a contemporary dancer, she performed the works of Anna Sokolow, Bill Evans, Shirley Ririe, H.T. Chen/Remy Charlip, Doug Hamby, Marcus Schulkind, Laurie Eisenhower, and others. After receiving her MFA from Arizona State University, she served on the dance faculties of Kansas State University, University of Oklahoma, Stephens College, Oakland University, and Seattle Pacific University. In 1993, she co-founded LEAVING GROUND/DANCE, a contemporary company, which toured throughout the U.S. and Canada. Since 2001, she has been on the faculty of Pacific Northwest Ballet School in Seattle. Her writing has been published in *Contact Quarterly* and at www.criticaldance.org. She may be reached at mcdermott910@gmail.com.